CONNIE CLARK

Spirited

LIVES

20 STORIES
of SAINTS
and their
AMAZING
& GIFTS &

TWENTY
THIRD 23rd
PUBLICATIONS
www.23rdpublications.com

TWENTY-THIRD PUBLICATIONS
A Division of Bayard
One Montauk Avenue, Suite 200
New London, CT 06320
(860) 437-3012 or (800) 321-0411
www.23rdpublications.com

ISBN: 978-1-62785-093-3
Library of Congress Control Number: 2015938705

Printed in the U.S.A.

Contents

HOW WILL YOU CHANGE THE WORLD?

If you'd met any of the people on these pages before their thrilling adventures began, they'd probably tell you they were nothing special. Most were poor. Many couldn't read or write. Some had done things they weren't proud of. And then a funny thing happened. God called them to do great things. They did their jobs so heroically and against so many odds that we remember them to this day. None of them did it alone. They had help from the Holy Spirit who brings us incredible gifts at baptism and confirmation.

These gifts show up in our actions, which we call the Fruits of the Holy Spirit. But they're not symbolic. They're very real. And to prove it, just look at the people on the following pages—ordinary folks like you and me. They just grabbed those superhuman, supernatural gifts and ran with them. Sure, they struggled and even doubted, but in the end, they accomplished great things.

So what about you? You may not believe it right now, but with the help of the Holy Spirit, you really can change the world. The gifts you've been given, or will receive, will get you there.

The Gifts of the Holy Spirit

....

 The Holy Spirit's seven gifts aren't like special powers that God zaps you with. They're not like superhero qualities that you can call on in emergencies, either. To understand them a little, imagine you're one of Jesus' apostles. Jesus has died and risen from the dead, and he's about to return to the Father. You're worried about what's next for you.

But Jesus knows exactly what you need. He promises that you won't be alone, because he will send a helper, an Advocate. That's the Holy Spirit, the third Person of the Holy Trinity, who comes to the apostles at the feast of Pentecost. They go out and change the world with the Good News of Jesus.

But back to you. You receive these same gifts at baptism and especially at confirmation. They are:

Wisdom ■ *Understanding* ■ *Counsel* ■ *Courage*

Knowledge ■ *Piety* ■ *Wonder and Awe*

Now there is one teensy catch. You have to allow these gifts to grow in you. You have to put them into practice. Sound tough? Take a look at how these ordinary people—whom we call saints, blesseds, and venerables—did it. They changed the world, and so can you.

5

1 Mary

ALL GOD'S GIFTS WRAPPED IN ONE PERFECT PACKAGE

So you're living your life, doing your best to be a good person, when suddenly everything gets turned upside down. Pregnant? The angel who brought the news never said anything about how you'd explain this to the man you're marrying. He didn't seem concerned with little details like what you'd say to your parents. Or how you'd raise a child as a single mom in a small town.

But you still said yes. Calmly, firmly, and with confidence in God's plan, you gave up all your plans and your future in the space of a minute. No resentment, no complaints. You didn't just put your life on hold. You gave it all, lock, stock, and barrel, to God.

How did Mary do it? The answer is wisdom. Not Albert Einstein genius-y kind of wisdom. Mary's is the kind of wisdom that recognizes another way of seeing things. The kind of wisdom that sees with God's eyes.

God's eyes? How can anyone presume to do that? Good question. We may not always understand God's plan, but like Mary, we always have a choice. We can say, "I don't get it, so I won't accept it." Or we can be like Mary and say, "I don't get it, but there's more to all of this than what I see." (OK, maybe she didn't exactly say it like that, but you get the picture.) Sure, Mary probably got scared—imagine seeing your grown son hanging on a cross! But through prayer and holy pondering, she glimpsed something much bigger at work.

Wisdom: Not about your SAT score

It's hard for us humans to grasp God's grace, so God gave us a young girl named Mary to help. Mary is an example of all the Holy Spirit's gifts at work, but that's really a lot for us to chew on at once, so we give her titles to help us understand one or two of her qualities at a time. One of those titles is Seat of Wisdom. You often see images of Mary seated on a chair or throne, holding baby Jesus, who basically *is* Wisdom, on her lap. You also see her, the sorrowful Pietà, holding her grown Son, who has just died on the cross, in her arms. For Mary to carry, bear, raise, and support the Son of God, she needed to see with God's eyes. She needed wisdom.

That kind of wisdom is the most important kind you can have. It doesn't come with a diploma; it comes with faith. In fact, theologians say wisdom is the *height* of faith. But don't worry: your faith doesn't have to be ironclad every minute of the day. You might have doubts. You might feel weak. It's OK. You just have to let the Holy Spirit in.

You can ask God outright for wisdom, the way King Solomon did. You can talk to Mary about it too. She knows exactly what you mean.

Something to think about

Have you ever been in Mary's shoes? Suddenly something happens that you can't understand? Write about it here—

what happened, how it made you feel, how it changed you. Then ask God to help you see it with his eyes, which are always the eyes of love.

_____

_____

_____

_____

Prayer

God, send me your Spirit and give me your wisdom so that I might learn to see with your eyes, feel with your heart, and speak with your words. Help me ponder Mary's life in the light of faith, that I might find true wisdom.

2 André of Montreal

ALWAYS AT THE DOOR

When you think of someone with great understanding, you might think of someone with a lot of education, like a doctor or a lawyer or a nuclear physicist. How about a man whose job was answering the door?

Brother André had little formal schooling, but he had an uncanny understanding of his fellow human beings. Maybe it came from the fact that he found himself alone and an orphan at age twelve. Maybe it was because he knew from experience what it meant be hungry and afraid.

Searching for work in Quebec and New England throughout his teens, he couldn't hold down a job because of poor health. When he appeared at the door of the Holy Cross Brothers, he carried a note from a priest friend that said, "I am sending you a saint."

The brothers took one look at this sickly youth and turned him down, giving him another hard lesson in disappointment and rejection. But eventually they accepted him, and he took vows in 1874 as a professed brother. Brother André was sent to a high school in Montreal to basically be the janitor and answer the door. He quipped, "When I joined this community, the superiors showed me the door, and I remained there forty years."

Brother André always knew what to say (or not to say) to visitors. People loved him. And there were the cures. Inspired by a devotion practiced in France, Brother André used plain lamp oil for the sick and wounded. He would tell people to pray to St. Joseph, and as a gesture of their faith, they should rub the oil on their wounds. But as word spread about cures and healings at the hands of Brother André, he refused to take any credit. "I do not cure," he said. "St. Joseph cures."

His own father's death when Brother André was a boy might explain his special connection to St. Joseph. And he wanted others to feel that connection too. So when Brother André had saved 200 dollars from nickels he'd collected for giving haircuts, he built a simple, one-room shrine to St. Joseph—a place where people could pray. Over time, Brother André watched his little room grow and expand. Today it's a huge basilica church in Montreal—St. Joseph's Oratory of Mt. Royal—where millions of people come to pray.

Understanding: When you just "get it"
Have you ever noticed that when you suddenly "get" something, it can come to you in a flash, almost out of nowhere? Pope Francis says the gift of understanding allows us to come into an "intimacy with God," which helps us understand things "as God understands them." That flash is the power of the Holy Spirit within you. When you see Jesus' life, death, and resurrection as part of a personal relation-

ship, and you want to express that by loving others as Jesus did, that's getting it. Brother André radiated joy as he spoke words of hope and cared for the sick. The man who said "My only ambition is to serve God in the most humble tasks" had true understanding. You can't study for that. You just have to let God in the door, just like Brother André did.

Something to think about

Do you know someone who gets you? Really and truly sees through it all and understands you? Hopefully, this person is a good, unselfish person who can see your many good qualities even when you can't. Jot down some of the good things this person might say about you.

_____

_____

_____

Prayer

Lord God, give me the gift of understanding,
that I might see you in everyone.

3 Pio of Pietrelcina
READER OF SOULS

In the remote town of San Giovanni Rotondo in southern Italy, a local Capuchin priest peered up a steep cliff. "A great hospital will be built there," he said. One of the men with him did a double take. "But, Padre, that's a mountain, with no roads. How would we get supplies?" One of the women chimed in. "This is a poor village, Padre. Where will we get the money? How will we do this?"

The padre shrugged. "Love," he said. "Just love." The people glanced at each other. Love was Padre's answer for everything, but building a hospital wasn't so simple.

The matter dropped, but the padre didn't forget. Years passed and World War II delayed things, but eventually he sought and received donations, often from unknown and unexpected sources, almost as if they came right out of the thin mountain air. He formed a committee, and an engineer presented blueprints. Later it was discovered this "engineer" had no qualifications, not even a degree. But the padre had some mysterious knowledge and hired him. Turns out the man was a genius. The hospital was completed in 1956 on the side of the steep mountain—an architectural marvel. It was just as the padre had predicted. The hospital, known as the House of Relief of Suffering, still serves the poor today and is considered one of the most advanced in Europe.

Knowledge: Really handy for moving mountains

True knowledge, the kind the Holy Spirit gives, is knowing that with God's love anything is possible, and anyone can accomplish anything. Put simply, knowledge is God's love in action. Padre Pio of Pietrelcina knew his hospital would be built, against all odds, against all common sense. When you have that kind of knowledge from the Holy Spirit, you can do anything, even when there's a mountain in the way.

Padre Pio had this same kind of knowledge about people. Take that genius engineer, for example. Or the thousands of people who came to him for confession. He told you if you were leaving something out, or what might be bothering you deep in your heart. Pio's amazing knowledge came with a price that included terrible suffering. He bore the stigmata, the five agonizing wounds of Christ, on his hands and feet and on his side. But Pio always radiated joy, and people just wanted to be near him. Countless stories are told of lives that were changed when people met God's reader of souls.

Something to think about

You probably won't have to suffer the way Pio did, but you might face impossible tasks in your life. What's difficult in your life right now? Is there a particular challenge or hurdle ahead? Write about it here. How might knowledge of God's incredible love for you help you meet this challenge?

_____

_____

_____

_____

Prayer

Lord God, St. Padre Pio is a powerful example of your love at work. Give me an understanding of your love, which surpasses everything. Help me use your love to change the world.

4 Thomas More

WHEN IT COMES TO GOD AND TRUTH, THERE'S JUST NO COMPROMISING

Power. Violence. Honor. It's not a slogan for a cable TV drama or a role-playing game. It was real life for the inner circle of King Henry VIII of England. Thomas More was a rising star in this high-stakes world where public servants could shoot to the top of the political food chain one day, only to have their heads roll down an executioner's plank the next.

It's a very complicated story, but the roller-coaster ride for Thomas began when King Henry wanted to divorce Queen Catherine so that he could marry Anne Boleyn. Henry asked the pope to annul his marriage. But after considering all the arguments, the pope said no. As a self-idolizing monarch, Henry was used to getting his own way. Not only did he reject the pope's ruling, but he made himself the supreme head of the church in England so that he could go ahead and end the marriage himself. He had a special document drawn up called the Oath of Supremacy. Anyone holding a high office had to sign it, swearing allegiance to the king as the head of the church. Refusing to sign the oath would be considered treason. Thomas, one of Henry's most trusted advisors, refused to sign, and quietly resigned.

In the modern world, Thomas would probably go off and write a tell-all memoir from his beachfront home in Mexico, but this was sixteenth-century England. The king sent Thomas to the Tower of London, hoping that imprisonment might bring him around. But Thomas, a brilliant lawyer and writer who once thought about becoming a monk, firmly believed the Bible carried more weight than Henry's marital whims. Jesus had appointed twelve apostles, and the Holy Spirit had given them the power to choose their successors, so in More's eyes, Henry was not only being sinful, he was leading the kingdom astray too. "No temporal man may be the head of the spirituality," Thomas said.

The rest of Henry's inner circle—and anyone in England who valued their life—went along with Henry. They gave Thomas plenty of chances to change his mind. At his trial for treason he was warned, "You see now how grievously you have offended his Majesty; yet he is so very merciful, that if you will lay aside your Obstinacy, and change your Opinion, we hope you may obtain Pardon and Favour in his sight."

Wasn't that nice of them? But Thomas couldn't go against his conscience. He was sentenced to death. Among his last words were these: "I die the king's faithful servant, but God's first."

Counsel: Your best decision-making tool

Pope Francis says counsel is "the gift by which the Holy Spirit makes our conscience capable of making a concrete choice in communion with God, according to the logic of Jesus and of his Gospel." The Spirit's gift of counsel is what we use when we make decisions based on what we know is morally right, even if those decisions are unpopular and cause us pain. Thomas More knew that his decision would cost him his life, but the Holy Spirit was with him, giving him peace. When he climbed the stairs at his execution, he was so peaceful that he cracked jokes. "I pray you, Mr. Lieutenant," he said, "see me safe up, and for my coming down, I can shift for myself."

Something to think about

People who speak moral truths can make everybody uncomfortable, especially if it means they have to give up something. Remember St. John the Baptist, who told Herod that he was being sinful? He ended up with the same fate as Thomas More. Can you think of a truth you believe in that goes against what society says is true? Or, to put it another way, is there something that society says is OK, but that you know in your heart Jesus would say is wrong? Write your thoughts here.

_____

_____

_____

_____

Prayer

Lord God, the truth can be hard to accept. Give me your gift of counsel so that I can always know the right course to take. Give me your strength that I might speak the truth, even when it comes at a high price to me.

5 Mary MacKillop
OUT IN THE WOOP WOOP WITH THE BROWN JOEYS

G'day, mates! Let's learn piety from a fair dinkum Brown Joey who traipsed around the Outback, didn't get a fair go, and never whinged about any of it. (Rough translation: Mother Mary MacKillop started an order of nuns who served the poor in remote corners of Australia. Misunderstood by some bishops, she was excommunicated but never complained once. That makes her a great example of someone with the gift of piety.)

Born in 1842 in Melbourne, Australia, Mary MacKillop wanted to serve the poor as a religious sister. In 1866 with the help of Father Julian Woods, she founded the Sisters of St. Joseph of the Sacred Heart, also known as the Josephites.

Woods helped Mary develop guidelines for the order. The sisters would go out in twos and threes to any woop woop (that's Aussie slang for a small, unimportant town) where they were needed. They lived among the poor without so much as a billy (teapot) of their own. Instead, they would rely on God's graciousness to support them.

Within a few years more than one hundred and twenty women joined the order. Known affectionately as "the brown joeys" (because their plain brown habits reminded Aussies of their beloved kangaroos), the sisters built schools, taught, ministered to the sick, and fed the hungry. It was tough, demanding, and often misunderstood work.

Remember, this was the 1870s, and women still didn't have the right to vote in Australia (or the rest of the world, for that matter). A few bishops couldn't wrap their minds around the idea of women working independently and felt the sisters should answer to a local priest or bishop, not to their religious order. When Mother Mary wrote to a bishop explaining everything, she was pretty gobsmacked (shocked) by the eventual response: she was excommunicated from the church. Crikey!

Mother Mary calmly obeyed the order, trusting as she always did in God's providence. Five months later, the order was lifted, and within a year, Rome officially recognized her Josephites. But Mary's troubles were far from over. Based on false evidence, some bishops believed she had a drinking problem and removed her from the order. Meanwhile, her old friend Fr. Woods saw the approval from Rome as a betrayal of their original ideals and refused to speak to her. And in the middle of all this, Mary's mother died. At one point, Mary wrote in her diary, "Cried myself to sleep. Was so weary of the struggle and felt so utterly alone. Could not pray or say my ordinary rosaries, only offered my weary heart's trials to my God with the wish that he would do his will and make of me what he pleased."

Eventually, Mother MacKillop was reinstated and led the order until her death in 1909. Today, her Josephites still work with the poorest of the poor wherever they see a need.

Mary MacKillop: Australian for piety, mate

Some people think of piety as acts of religious devotion. But it's important to understand the heart of this gift is loyalty to God and the things of God. Truly pious people like Mary MacKillop see God not just as the creator of the universe, but also as a loving Father. They want to share this loving, compassionate God with the whole world.

Something to think about

Some people say religion should be kept in church. But Catholics don't buy that. Following Jesus means we love our brothers and sisters just as Jesus did. That's why you see the church leading the way in humanitarian relief. We also run hospitals, schools, and orphanages, feed the hungry, clothe the naked, and fight for human rights all over the world. This is how we are loyal to God. Think of one big way you can be loyal to God, and one small way. Write them down here.

_____

_____

_____

_____

Prayer

God, I know you are calling me to help others in your name. Give me the gift of piety so that I might act with love and justice toward all.

6 Maximilian Kolbe

PATRON OF A DIFFICULT CENTURY

A prisoner had escaped. So by the fiendish logic of the Auschwitz death camp, a lesson needed to be taught. Ten other prisoners were randomly chosen to die, painfully and slowly. As the commandant made his selections, one of the doomed men pleaded in desperation, "My poor wife! My children! What will they do?"

Suddenly another prisoner shuffled forward and stood at attention. "I am a Catholic priest," he said. "Let me take his place. I am old. He has a wife and children."

The commandant paused. We'll never know what stopped him from shooting both men on the spot, but the young man's life was spared. In his place, Father Maximilian Kolbe, Prisoner 16770, walked with the other men to an underground bunker where they would be deprived of food and water until they died.

Witnesses outside Cell Block 13 reported hearing Fr. Kolbe inside, leading the men in prayers, the Rosary, and singing. Within days, the singing turned to ghostly whispering, and at the end of two weeks, Fr. Kolbe was the only man still alive. The bunker was needed, so the guards gave him a lethal injection. It's reported that, in death, Fr. Kolbe's face was calm and radiant.

Born in 1894 in Poland, Fr. Maximilian Kolbe was a Conventual Franciscan Friar. Despite losing a lung to tuberculosis, he traveled to Japan as a missionary, founded a crusade to honor Mary, and ran a small Catholic radio station and printing press. In 1941, he was arrested in Warsaw and later sent to Auschwitz. Singled out for harsh treatment, he still managed to hear confessions, minister to the dying, share his meager food portions, and reassure inmates about the love of God.

Where did Fr. Kolbe get his courage and strength? Read one of his letters for a clue:

> *Dear Mama,*
> *At the end of the month of May I was*
> *transferred to the camp of Auschwitz.*
> *Everything is well in my regard. Be*
> *tranquil about me and about my health,*
> *because the good God is everywhere and*
> *provides for everything with love...*

Fr. Kolbe was canonized in 1982. Even before that, in 1979, Pope St. John Paul II had declared him to be "the patron of our difficult century." Today, whenever we see hatred, injustice, or senseless death, we can think of Fr. Kolbe, who never lost his faith in the power of God's love.

Courage (Fortitude): No greater love
Jesus said, "No one has greater love than this, to lay down

one's life for one's friends" (John 15:13). Through the Spirit's gift of fortitude, we receive the strength to love when it is most difficult and harrowing. Fortitude helps us see past our weaknesses and limitations, but Pope Francis reminds us that we need fortitude more often than we might think. "For most of us," he says, "the gift of fortitude is exercised in our patient pursuit of holiness in the circumstances of our daily lives."

You might need fortitude to face a difficult person or situation. It helps to remember that no one can really harm who you are—that is, harm your very soul.

Something to think about

We often hear people blaming religion for wars and violence in the world. What do you think Jesus would say about that? Write your thoughts here.

_____

_____

_____

_____

Prayer

Lord God, when I get weary and discouraged,
send your spirit to refresh my soul and guide my actions
with love for you. I pray especially for all who are persecuted
and martyred for their faith. Give them your courage
and help them show the world your great love.

7 **Francis of Assisi**
MAN OF POVERTY, PEACE, AND ALL CREATION

"Don't forget the poor." The soon-to-be-elected pope was stunned at the timing of the words whispered in his ear by an old friend, a fellow cardinal. It was if Jesus himself had spoken. So he chose the name of St. Francis of Assisi as his papal name, to remind everyone about "the man of poverty, the man of peace, the man who loves and protects creation."

Pope Francis' namesake, Francis of Assisi, had a similar experience once. Praying in an old chapel, he heard a voice saying, "Go, Francis, and repair my house, which as you see is falling into ruin." Francis thought the voice was referring to the little chapel and set out to rebuild it.

First, Francis hightailed it to his father's business, where he grabbed a horse and some expensive cloth. He sold those, intending to use the money to rebuild the little chapel. When Francis' dad found out, he was beyond furious. He yelled. He screamed. He locked Francis in a family jail (yes, rich people had those in the thirteenth century). As a final touch, he publicly humiliated Francis by dragging him before the bishop. Francis' reaction is hard to believe, but it's true: he stripped off all of his clothes as a sign that he would no longer have anything to do with his father or his father's money. The only Father he would honor was the one to whom he said, "Our Father."

With that, Francis walked away from his former life. He wore the clothes of the poor—a ragged brown tunic with a rope tied around the middle. He began preaching about the love of God. Some thought he was crazy, but soon he had a huge following.

Later on, Francis realized the voice he'd heard was telling him about the greater church, which at the time had lost its way. Francis had a bigger mission. He trekked across the Italian countryside, preaching about the need for penance, love, and peace. His powerful words and austere way of life attracted thousands of followers; they became known as the Franciscan Friars.

Wonder and Awe: How can you not be amazed?

If you met Francis personally you'd see that he was different. Not just because of his moth-eaten clothes or even the stigmata, the five wounds of Christ, that he received. You would have felt closer to God just being with Francis, as if he were in God's presence at all times. And he was, because Francis saw and experienced God in all things and in all people. This interconnectedness inspired him to write the beautiful Canticle of the Sun near the end of his life:

> *Be praised, my Lord,*
> *through all Your creatures,*
> *especially through my lord Brother Sun,*
> *who brings the day;*
> *and You give light through him.*

And he is beautiful and radiant
in all his splendor!
Of You, Most High, he bears the likeness...

The Spirit's gift of wonder and awe is also known as "fear of the Lord." That doesn't mean being scared of God. It means respecting the power of God in creation and not wanting to do anything that would turn you away from his great love.

Francis' wonder and awe was a tad more intense than most people's, but it doesn't mean that when you find yourself speechless at the sight of a soaring eagle, or in wonder at the beauty of a child, the Holy Spirit isn't working within you too.

Something to think about

How many times this week have you just stared at something? Your phone, the TV, your bedroom wall...What if you took two minutes to stare at a part of God's creation? Do that today. Write down what you see. Then speak to God about it.

_____

_____

_____

_____

Prayer

God, give me a few moments each day to experience the wonder and awe of your creation. Holy Spirit, give me the gift of seeing beauty everywhere, especially in the poor, sick, and elderly.

The Fruits of the Holy Spirit

SEEING IT ALL WITH YOUR OWN EYES

 You probably won't see a dove descending at a baby's baptism, or tongues of fire at confirmation. But you can see the Gifts of the Holy Spirit at work in people. Here's what Jesus says:

Just so, every good tree bears good fruit, and a rotten tree bears bad fruit. A good tree cannot bear bad fruit, nor can a rotten tree bear good fruit. Every tree that does not bear good fruit will be cut down and thrown into the fire. So by their fruits you will know them. (Matthew 7:17–20)

The Fruits of the Holy Spirit are the observable behaviors of people who live the Gifts of the Holy Spirit. You might say these fruits are the Holy Spirit in action. They are:

Charity (Love) ▪ *Joy* ▪ *Peace* ▪ *Patience* ▪ *Kindness*
Goodness ▪ *Generosity* ▪ *Gentleness* ▪ *Faithfulness*
Modesty ▪ *Self-control* ▪ *Chastity (Purity)*

In other words, people who fully live the Holy Spirit's gifts are people who live life to the fullest—the way almighty God intends. Now you might be wondering, does that mean that only people who are baptized and confirmed are capable of giving love or spreading kindness? Of course not. But notice we say *fully* living God's gifts. The sacraments help you really live the life God has planned for you. Fully and completely, no holds barred.

In some people, the Fruits of the Holy Spirit are really obvious. Think Mother Teresa or Pope Francis. Then again, some people, like Thérèse of Lisieux or Matt Talbot, are so quiet about it, we don't know the full extent of their incredible lives until after they're gone. But one thing is true for all people who really and truly live the Fruits of the Holy Spirit. They are people you are naturally drawn to. They have a charisma and joy about them because they are filled with God's true and perfect love. They may struggle and have tough times, but they are people you can't help but love. And I'm betting you're one of them.

8 Thérèse of Lisieux
LITTLE HERO OF LOVE

The fidgeting was driving Thérèse crazy. In the pew behind her, a nun tapped her foot, fiddled with rosary beads, flipped through prayer books, and smoothed out her habit. (Even *that* was noisy.) She coughed. She wriggled. She squirmed. She sighed. She sneezed. Could she ever keep still?

"I wanted to turn around and glare at the culprit to make her be quiet," Thérèse wrote in her diary. But no, she told herself. The nun has feelings. So with perspiration dripping down her face, Thérèse tried to endure the shuffling and fussing behind her. "My prayer was nothing more than the prayer of suffering," she wrote. Then inspiration hit. "It was impossible not to hear it, so I turned my attention to listening really closely to it, as if it were a magnificent concert, and spent the rest of the time offering it to Jesus. It was certainly not the prayer of quiet!"

For Thérèse, who was hypersensitive to noise, this minor incident cost her greatly. It might seem trivial, but that's the message of St. Thérèse of Lisieux. Our smallest, least noticed acts of love have immense value to God. Even one short moment can be heroic.

Thérèse recorded these moments, which she referred to as her "little way," in her journals, which were themselves courageous acts of love. Bewildered by the request from her superior to begin a journal, and unsure of how she would do it when she was often too sick to hold a pen, Thérèse started writing—for love of her superior and of God.

Her journals, later published under the title *The Story of a Soul*, have sold millions of copies. She tells how she went from a spoiled French girl to a Carmelite nun, and how she developed her hidden life of love and prayer. Thérèse somehow knew that her days were growing shorter—she died at age twenty-four—but that her hidden life would go on. "After my death, I will let fall a shower of roses," she said. "I will spend my heaven doing good upon earth."

Charity: The "little way" of love goes a long way

You can't get to the fruits and gifts of the Spirit by going a purely human route. Real love comes from God. And since God created us as unique individuals, he knows love works differently—and beautifully—for all of us. We're not all called to begin religious orders like Francis of Assisi, or to give our lives like Fr. Kolbe. But every single one of us is called to love God above all things. Maybe you kept your mouth shut instead of making a sarcastic remark to a friend who let you down. Maybe you let someone borrow your phone when their battery ran out. Or maybe you've chosen to follow a career path of service. You may never know what sort of chain reaction comes from your smallest acts of love, but St. Thérèse wants you to know that God sees it all. And he loves you more than you can imagine.

Something to think about

Name one person you care about. Write down three small things you can do today to show this person your love.

_____

_____

_____

_____

Prayer

O God, sometimes I think our world has lost its understanding of what love truly is. Show me, every day, every moment, what I can do to love each person as you love them.

9 Josephine Bakhita
LUCK HAS NOTHING TO DO WITH IT

She was eight years old with no concept of stranger danger. So on an afternoon in 1877, when a man she didn't know approached her as she walked from her village in Sudan, the girl thought she was doing the right thing by obeying him. The stranger told her to go into a nearby grove and bring him some fruit. She sprinted off, and her peaceful, carefree childhood disappeared with her into the trees.

Ambushed by knife-wielding slave traders, the little girl was taken from her village, starved, and forced to walk barefoot for hundreds of miles. The trauma of her kidnapping made the girl forget her own name. One of her captors sarcastically called her Bakhita, which means "lucky." Bought and sold many times in the markets of North Africa, she endured years of beatings and a kind of forced cutting before she was finally presented as a "gift" to an Italian family. When the family moved, they sent Bakhita and one of their children to stay temporarily at a convent in Venice. It was there that Bakhita began hearing about God, and when her "master" returned for her, Bakhita refused to leave. The master and his wife were outraged, but the convent's mother superior went to the authorities, and in 1889 an Italian court ruled that Bakhita's slavery had been illegal from the beginning.

Now in her twenties, Bakhita was finally free and in control of her own life. She chose to stay at the convent, where she was baptized and later became a sister herself, taking the name Josephine Margaret and Fortunata, which is Latin for lucky. As a sister she was assigned to a convent in northern Italy, where she lived quietly. But people noticed her tranquil charisma, gentle voice, and calming ways. During World War II, the citizens of her town said they felt protected by her very presence, and it's a fact that no bombs fell there. Look at a photograph of Sr. Josephine and you'll understand what everyone meant. It's hard to not be captivated by her peaceful, loving smile.

Joy: The real thing

After all she had been through, Sister Josephine could have been excused for retiring into a private world of grief over her lost youth, and of bitterness over her suffering. But she showed the world that nothing can conquer the joy of the Holy Spirit. Not only did she lead a life of joy; she shared it with others.

When someone asked what she would do if she met her kidnappers, Josephine surprised everyone with her forgiving answer. "I would kneel and kiss their hands. For, if these things had not happened, I would not have been a Christian and a religious today."

Something to think about

Why do bad things happen to good people? If you've ever wondered that, you're not alone. People ask that question all the time. Sometimes their answer is to blame someone or something. Or God. Playing the "blame game" might give us a little bit of satisfaction for a while, but it ultimately leads to anger, frustration, and a need to "get back" at whoever is at fault. It helps to remember that Jesus was the ultimate good person—and a very bad thing happened to him. But out of his suffering and death came new life and joy for the entire human race. It didn't happen because God wanted to hurt his own Son, but because God loves us incredibly. When bad things happen to you, or when you see some evil in the world, what can you remember about Jesus and his love for you? Write it down here.

_____

_____

_____

_____

Prayer

God, I ask you to give your world the understanding that true joy can only be found through you. Help me share your love with those who are suffering and feeling unloved today.

10 Blessed Franz Jägerstätter
SACRIFICING EVERYTHING FOR GOD

When Adolph Hitler's motorcade drove into Vienna in 1938, more than 200,000 German and Austrian citizens turned out, waving Nazi flags and welcoming him. Days later, when Germany annexed Austria, many citizens overwhelmingly approved of what seemed to be a bloodless, peaceful take-over. Most Austrians looked forward to a prosperous future under the new regime. More than seventy years after World War II, it's hard for us to comprehend how so many people could turn a blind eye to Hitler. But one man didn't go along with everyone else and saw the Nazis for what they were. And he paid a terrible price.

Franz Jägerstätter was a simple Austrian farmer, struggling to support his family of four. A strong Catholic, he was active in his parish, but when he began to complain about Hitler, friends and neighbors began to shun him. When the Nazi party set up a family assistance program in his village, Franz turned it down—even though it would have made a big difference for his family.

Then Franz had to make the biggest decision of his life.

Should he sign up for Hitler's army, like the other men of his village? Like all loyal Austrian men? Of course he should, friends and neighbors said. He had to support his family, and he had a responsibility to obey legitimate authorities.

But Franz didn't agree. Sure, in a normal world, obedience to authority was the right course. But no one around him seemed to recognize the evil that was settling into Austria and so much of Europe.

Franz did not show up for active duty, declaring himself a conscientious objector. The Nazis did not tolerate disobedience, and he was thrown in prison. Even his wife at first begged him to rethink his decision. Were his convictions more important than his family? If he were to die in prison, what would become of them?

Peace: It begins within you

Franz was criticized by friends and neighbors, including his fellow Catholics, for failing to support his family. But Franz wrote, "Everyone tells me, of course, that I should not do what I am doing because of the danger of death. I believe it is better to sacrifice one's life right away than to place oneself in the grave danger of committing sin and then dying."

Eventually his wife, who dearly loved her husband, understood. She and her children supported Franz to the end. He was given a military trial and sentenced to death. On August 9, 1943, Franz Jägerstätter was executed by guillotine.

But even after his death, Franz was criticized. His name was left off the village war memorial, and it took several years before his widow received her pension. In 1964, an American sociologist researched and wrote *In Solitary*

Witness, a book about Franz. He was beatified by the church in 2007. Today, Franz is honored around the world as a man who understood that peace is more than a word; it's a sacrifice and a way of life.

Something to think about

Jesus says, "Blessed are the peacemakers, for they shall be called children of God" (Matthew 5:9). We are called to be peacemakers everywhere. So, how are you a peacemaker in your family? At school? Among your friends? In your community? In the world at large? Write down the ways you will be a peacemaker in all these places.

_____

_____

_____

_____

Prayer

O Jesus, you said, "Peace I leave with you;
my peace I give to you. Not as the world gives do I give it
to you." Help me to understand and live your peace.

11 Bernadette Soubirous
ALWAYS TRUE TO MARY

Some people said she was mentally ill. Others insisted she was trying to make money. Or both. Despite public opinion, Bernadette maintained an almost otherworldly peace throughout her life. When people jeered at her, tugged at her clothes, or even slapped her across the face (oh yes, they did), Bernadette remained true to her story about *Aquero*—the young girl who appeared to her in a tiny cave in Lourdes, France.

You'd think that if Mary appeared to you as she did to Bernadette, your life would be happy and full of peace. But for Bernadette it was just the opposite. It all started when Bernadette was fourteen. Collecting firewood outside the town of Lourdes, France, in 1858, she heard the sound of rushing wind. Looking up she saw a dazzling light from a nearby cave. Inside, a beautiful young girl appeared, bathed in light. Bernadette, who was from a poor family with little education, could only describe the girl as *Aquero*, which is loosely translated as "that." She just had no words to describe the young woman's heavenly beauty. For about a month, Bernadette visited the cave almost daily. The lady, as Bernadette also called her, spoke about the world's need for prayer, penance, and the kind of poverty of spirit Jesus talked about in the Beatitudes (Matthew 5:3). As word of the vision spread, great crowds followed Bernadette. Some didn't believe her; others demanded that she ask the lady for special favors.

Bernadette said the lady wanted a chapel built on the site. Once during one of Bernadette's visions, people saw her scratching at the ground. A trickle of water emerged and, by the next day, a stream of clear water flowed through the area. Today, the spring of Lourdes is a place of hope and miraculous spiritual and physical healing for millions of people every year. The place where the lady told Bernadette that she was the Immaculate Conception is now the Sanctuary of Our Lady of Lourdes.

Patience: "I cannot promise you happiness in this life, only in the next"

But back to Bernadette. Her visits with the lady filled her with indescribable peace and joy. But no one else did. An endless stream of doctors, police, and clergy questioned her. They even examined her eyes and tested her reflexes during the apparitions. Even her own family members harassed her. Long after the visions ended, Bernadette still received more attention than she wanted. So in 1866, Bernadette joined the Sisters of Notre Dame. For a while, she even had harsh treatment there. But she remembered something the lady had told her: "I cannot promise you happiness in this life, only in the next."

Now those are tough words to hear! But Bernadette accepted it joyfully, knowing that eternal happiness was going to last a lot longer than the suffering she had to put up with.

Bernadette remained hidden from the world in the convent until her death in 1879. Her incorrupt body lies in a glass casket in France, where people still stare at her. But this saint's patience is eternal.

Something to think about

Is there someone who's really been bugging you lately? Someone at school? A teacher? Your brother or sister? Write your thoughts about it here. Finish by asking God to give you patience and understanding with this person.

_____

_____

_____

_____

Prayer

O God, you gave Bernadette endless patience to deal with the important message you had for the world at Lourdes. What messages do you have for me? Give me patience with the noise and distractions of the world so that I can be calm enough to hear your voice.

12 María Guadalupe García Zavala

SAINT IN THE MIDST OF VIOLENCE

The midnight knock at the door was so sharp and sudden that one of the sisters nearly dropped a bottle of medicine. Up and down the ward the other sisters froze. Would Madre Lupita answer the door?

As the knocking grew louder, the nuns crossed themselves. The city of Guadalajara, Mexico, was a battleground in 1926, and the Catholic Church was considered the enemy. Just last week there'd been a violent shootout inside Our Lady of Guadalupe church. Eighteen men had been killed near the altar. What was to stop those government soldiers from coming to the hospital and opening fire here?

The knocking continued and everyone's attention turned to one nun, sitting at a patient's bedside. Finally, Madre Lupita stood. "It's Christ," she said. "He's coming to see us."

She disappeared down the hall. "Our Father, who art in heaven..." the sisters prayed. They heard the front door open, and Madre Lupita's voice directing a novice to get hot water and bandages. The nurses sighed with relief. Another patient. They could deal with that...

Kindness: "Be poor with the poor"

María Guadalupe García Zavala, known as Madre Lupita, was no stranger to violence and danger. During the government crackdown on religion in the 1920s in Mexico, many Catholics were martyred, including Blessed Miguel Pro, a Jesuit priest. Madre Lupita often had to hide priests in the little hospital.

Her kindness was well known, along with her motto: "Be poor with the poor." Madre Lupita didn't see differences between enemies and friends, rich and poor. Everyone was welcome.

At her canonization in 2013, Pope Francis said that Madre Lupita's example should encourage people not to "get wrapped up in themselves, their own problems, their own ideas, their own interests, but to go out and meet those who need attention, help, and other assistance."

Something to think about

Jesus reminds us to be kind to everyone, and not just people we like. "For if you love those who love you, what recompense will you have?" (Matthew 5:46). Who is someone you might not like, but to whom you need to be kind today? Write down some ideas.

_____

_____

_____

Prayer

*O God, your kindness knows no limits. Help me
today, so that I may be kind to everyone I meet.*

13 Blessed Pier Giorgio Frassati

FEW BUT GOOD, LIKE MACARONI

"We are few, but we are good, like macaroni." That kind of motto could only come from the mind of Pier Giorgio Frassati. Handsome, athletic, and known for practical jokes, Frassati loved to laugh and goof around with his friends, but he wasn't afraid to express how deeply he cared for them.

So in his early twenties, as his friends began going their separate ways, he created the Tipi Loschi Society. That's Italian for "swindlers and swindlerettes" or "shady characters." The name was ironic because Frassati was anything but shady. He invited friends to daily Mass with him and would gladly empty his pockets for anyone who needed money. His Tipi Loschi friends—a few young men and women from his Italian town of Turin—got together regularly to hike or climb the Italian Alps. And, of course, they prayed. Pier Giorgio felt prayer and mutual support would see them through the challenges of early adulthood. Yes, they were few, but they were very good. And maybe a little crazy too. In a good way.

Pier Giorgio was born on Holy Saturday in Turin, Italy, in 1901. At seventeen, he joined the St. Vincent De Paul Society, where he cared for the sick and needy, joked and played with orphans, and helped servicemen returning from World War I. Frassati spoke naturally and conversationally about faith with anyone. He wasn't preachy, just passionate and fun about his love for God. Once when he lost a bet with a friend, he sent her a book of St. Paul's letters. When his best friend, Marco, joined the Air Force, Pier Giorgio sent him a blessing.

Goodness: Toward the top

One of the last photos of Pier Giorgio was taken as he climbed his beloved Alps. He scrawled a caption on the picture: "verso l'alto," which means "toward the top." Although it wasn't his personal motto, the expression captures everything that Pier Giorgio was about—always striving for goodness and perfection.

Just before graduating from college, Pier Giorgio came down with polio. Even in his last moments, he cared for the poor and sick. The day before he died, at age 24, he scribbled a message to a friend asking him to take medicine to an impoverished man he'd been caring for. At Pier Giorgio's funeral, thousands of people from all over Italy turned out. His parents were shocked. They had no idea their son had touched so many lives.

Pier Giorgio was beatified by Pope St. John Paul II, who called him the "Man of the Eight Beatitudes." The message to us is that there is room in every life of goodness for plenty of fun. And a lot of macaroni.

Something to think about

Pier Giorgio Frassati was a practical joker who was known

for things like shortchanging sheets of friends and even a few priests. But he also went to daily Mass, served the poor, and read about the saints. How might you be inspired by Pier Giorgio to combine a life of goodness with a life of fun? Write down something you are passionate about—a sport, a hobby, anything important to you. Come up with some ideas for how you can make it a way to praise God or be of service to others.

_____

_____

_____

_____

Prayer
O God, I accept your call to goodness.
Make me a sign of your love to the whole world.

14 John XXIII
GOOD POPE JOHN

Angelo wasn't supposed to do anything. Men who were elected pope in their late seventies might give blessings and write nice homilies, but they weren't supposed to make waves. But for Angelo, the Holy Spirit had other ideas. Taking the name John XXIII, Angelo didn't just make waves; he changed history.

The ecumenical council that John called, known as Vatican II, was the largest meeting held in human history, with more than 2500 priests, bishops, theologians, and even representatives from other religions attending. It changed the way you and I attend the Mass. It helped the church respond to the challenges of the modern world. It was one of the greatest accomplishments of the church in hundreds of years, but Pope John didn't even live to see it completed. He died in 1963 while the Council was on a break.

John XXIII, known as Good Pope John, did a lot of other things popes weren't supposed to do. Without telling anyone, he would sneak away from the Vatican and stroll around Rome as just another simple priest. He played papal pranks—rigging the sprinklers in the papal gardens to turn on just when his friends were visiting. He was famous for one-liners: "How many people work at the Vatican?" a reporter once asked. "Oh, no more than half of them," John answered with a sly wink.

Generosity: Self-giving love

Coming from a family of fourteen children, Pope John really understood how to give of himself. Before being elected pope, he was a diplomat and figured out a way to rig visas and other documents so that thousands of Jews could escape Nazi Germany.

Still, John didn't want people to think of him as anything special. He once talked about the problem of making saints bigger than they are. What was really important, he said, was love. Self-giving love.

When he gave his notes and journals to an assistant, he said, "My soul is in these pages. I was a good, innocent boy, a little timid. I wanted to love God at all costs and I thought of nothing other than becoming a priest at the service of simple souls in need of patient and diligent care."

Something to think about

Who do you need to be more generous with today? Write down the first name that comes to your mind and decide what you will do to be good to them.

_____

_____

_____

Prayer

O God, today, don't let me forget to be generous.

15 Paul
UM...GENTLENESS? REALLY?

Before his conversion, Paul was a self-righteous Pharisee named Saul who ran around persecuting Jesus' followers. But after being blinded, converted, and baptized, Paul became a powerful force *for* Jesus, preaching, writing, and building up the church. He was imprisoned, scourged, stoned, and shipwrecked. Christianity owes a lot to Paul, who traveled all over the known world, spreading the Good News of Jesus.

That's all great, but gentleness? Really?

Paul might sound more like a cyclone of activity than a gentle breeze of peace. But the Holy Spirit's gift of gentleness isn't about being timid or passive. It's about letting the Spirit take hold of you and going where God sends you. Gentle people are free of inward conflict because they use their gifts and talents the way God intends. They might be bold, or they might be quiet, but they don't ignore their gifts, or fight them. They often leave attachments behind—things like sin, resentments, even comforts—and calmly pick up their cross with Jesus, trusting that God will see them through.

Gentleness: The secret to happiness

Before his conversion and baptism, Saul fought the move-
ment of the Spirit, keeping himself closed tight like a fist. He
had breathed "murderous threats" against Jesus' followers.
(Does that sound like someone who is happy to you?) Once,
while on his way to Damascus, a brilliant light flashed around
Saul, and he fell to the ground. A voice spoke: "Saul, Saul,
why are you persecuting me?" Blinded, Saul asked, "Who are
you, sir?" The voice answered that it was Jesus, "whom you
are persecuting." Jesus told him to go on to the city. "You will
be told what you must do" (Acts 9:1–6). Remember, this was
Saul, who had been putting people in chains for following
Jesus. Now Jesus was telling him what to do. *And now Saul
did it.* Willingly. He even had to be "led by the hand." Can
you imagine letting everything go, and letting yourself be led
blindly (literally) into an unknown situation?

With no idea of what was ahead, Saul stayed in the city
for three days, ate nothing, and prayed. Then he allowed one
of Jesus' followers, a man named Ananias, to lay his hands
on him. "Brother Saul," Ananias said, "the Lord Jesus who
appeared to you on the road has sent me that you may regain
your sight and be filled with the Holy Spirit" (Acts 9:17). Saul
was cured of his blindness and baptized. He was a different
man, with a new name, Paul, given to him by God. He wrote
things like this: "Therefore, I am content with weaknesses,
insults, hardships, persecutions, and constraints, for the
sake of Christ; for when I am weak, then I am strong" (2
Corinthians 12:10).

Look at the difference between Saul and Paul. Saul is the
exact opposite of gentleness, fighting against the Spirit. But

for Paul, it didn't matter if he was in jail or shipwrecked; he was content. In fact, he wrote some of his most joyful letters while in prison, in chains, or under arrest. This kind of gentleness gives us confidence that in any situation, no matter how hopeless, God will see us through. We never face our problems alone. We just have to be gentle and let the Holy Spirit—through Christ within us—strengthen us and show us the way. That's the way to happiness.

Something to think about

Paul wrote, "The fruit of the Spirit is love, joy, peace, patience, kindness, generosity, faithfulness, gentleness, self-control. Against such there is no law" (Galatians 5:22–23). Thinking about gentleness in particular, what do you think Paul means when he says that "against such there is no law"? Write your thoughts here.

Prayer

Jesus, help me relax as I come into your presence.
Help me be comfortable with you, and completely myself.
Send your Spirit of gentleness into my life so that I may
discover and accept my true self. Then, lifted by your
power, may I follow the path you have set out for me.

16 Joan of Arc
TEENAGE HERO

To anyone who thinks you have to wait until you're older to do anything really important, I give you Joan of Arc. At fourteen, with no military experience and unable to read or write, she commanded the king of France and an entire army. Dozens of movies and books have been made about her. Even Mark Twain, who wrote *The Adventures of Tom Sawyer*, and who was no fan of the church or saintly people, spent more than a decade researching her short but adventurous life and writing what he considered his most important work, *Personal Recollections of Joan of Arc*. So who was this teenage girl who has fascinated and inspired so many generations of people around the world?

Born in France in 1412, at the height of the Hundred Years' War with England, Joan began having visions of three saints when she was twelve years old. At first, she said, Michael the Archangel, Catherine, and Margaret simply told her to be good, attend Mass, and live a holy life. Within two years, they directed her to take up a crusade to save France. She made her way to the court of Charles VII, the king of France, and convinced him to allow her to lead an army. Her battles are the stuff of legend—except they really happened. The most famous, the siege at Orleans, turned the tide of a long war in France's favor, and set in motion the events that ended English occupation of parts of the country. So it's easy to see why Saint Joan of Arc is a national hero and patron saint of France.

Even in battle, Joan held fast to her faith. She ordered the most hardened of French soldiers to stop using foul language—and they did. When an arrow struck her, driving six inches into her shoulder, she refused the soldiers' good luck charms, saying she would rather die than commit a sin. Then *she pulled the arrow out herself.* All through her campaigns, she never missed Mass or the opportunity to go to confession. Ultimately, Charles betrayed her and Joan was captured in battle. Caught in a web of politics of which she was completely innocent, she was tried in court and steadfastly affirmed that the voices she heard were from God. She was burned at the stake for heresy on May 30, 1431. Joan was 19. At her request, a cross was held up for her to look at, and as she died, she cried out Jesus' name. It wasn't until a quarter of a century after her death that she was pronounced innocent and a martyr.

Faithfulness: Not about hearing angelic voices
People often think Joan was canonized because she was a hero in France, or because she was a mystic who heard the voices of saints. But Joan was canonized for her sanctity and obedience to God's will. She accepted the job God gave her with joy and a positive outlook that spread to everyone around her, even the judges at her trial. You've probably

heard dozens of times that with faith, you can accomplish anything, but Joan shows that with the help of the Holy Spirit, you can change the course of history.

Something to think about

Mary, Joan of Arc, and Bernadette were all about the same age when they received messages from God. Why do you think God chooses to speak to so many young people? Write your thoughts here.

_____

_____

_____

_____

Prayer

God, give me faithfulness like Saint Joan so that I may always stand up for what is right.

17 Joseph
FRIEND TO THE END

How could she do this? Mary was the perfect girl—kind, pure, intelligent, beautiful. Now she was throwing everything away—her reputation, her future, *their* future together—Joseph and Mary's. How could she do this?

We don't know how long Joseph must have agonized over Mary and the baby she carried, but we can imagine how he felt when he first heard the news. Confused, probably. Betrayed, conflicted, sad, angry. And what was Joseph supposed to do? He could have had Mary publicly humiliated. People in his time lived with a brutal sense of justice. So no one would have blinked an eye over a very public persecution of Mary. It would have been as accepted as today's reality court TV: "The court is now in session. All rise for the public stoning of Mary of Nazareth..."

But Joseph wasn't that kind of man. Even though he was probably terribly hurt and disappointed, he wanted to spare Mary: "Joseph her husband," Matthew's gospel tells us, "since he was a righteous man, yet unwilling to expose her to shame, decided to divorce her quietly" (Matthew 1:19).

He was a righteous man. Joseph was also a modest man. The *Catechism of the Catholic Church* gives us a beautiful definition of what it means to be modest:

> *Modesty protects the intimate center of the person. It means refusing to unveil what should remain hidden. It guides how one looks at others and behaves toward them in conformity with the dignity of persons and their solidarity...Modesty is decency.*
>
> (NOS. 2521–2522)

Joseph wanted to protect Mary, despite what he thought she might have done. And he made this generous and merciful decision even before the angel came to him in a dream:

"Joseph, son of David, do not be afraid to take Mary your wife into your home. For it is through the holy Spirit that this child has been conceived in her. She will bear a son and you are to name him Jesus, because he will save his people from their sins." (Matthew 1:20–21)

Modesty: Seeing the dignity in everyone

So Joseph's problem was solved, but another bigger one replaced it. Ever feel intimidated? Imagine how you'd feel if you were the foster parent of the Son of God. What if something happened to the baby on your watch? But Joseph accepted his role quietly, humbly, and modestly. If you want to know what modesty is, think of Joseph protecting the child Jesus and loving him as a father would. Think of Joseph departing from this life when his time came. Not questioning

it. Not complaining. Think of Joseph, and you'll understand
modesty and much, much more.

Something to think about

Is there someone in your life who you think has overlooked
you? What about other people? Could there be someone out
there who needs your attention too? Think about it. Write
your thoughts here.

_____

_____

_____

_____

Prayer

_Lord God, I am created by you in your great goodness. Help me to
respect the dignity of all people, including me. Give me modesty, that
I may, like St. Joseph, treat everyone with decency and fairness._

18 Venerable Matt Talbot

GOD'S LOVE IS STRONGER THAN ANY ADDICTION

The story of Matt Talbot isn't just about overcoming addiction. It's about accepting the strength of the Holy Spirit so that you can accomplish greatness—no matter what the voices in your head tell you.

Matt was born into the monstrous poverty of Dublin, Ireland, in the late nineteenth century. Like most impoverished Irish children, he dropped out of school to seek work. By all accounts he was a hard worker and generous to a fault.

But there was another side to Matt. Like so many others trying to forget the misery and shame of poverty, Matt drank. By the time he was sixteen, he suffered from alcohol addiction, spending most or all of his pay on booze. One evening, completely broke and out of credit, he waited outside a pub for someone to buy him a drink. Friends came and went but no one invited him inside. Dejected and angry, Matt stumbled home and announced to his mother that he was going to "take the pledge" and abstain from alcohol.

Matt's mom looked him in the eye and said, "Go, in God's name, but don't take it unless you are going to keep it." (At the time, people didn't yet understand that addiction is a disease, and not a lack of willpower.) As Matt left, she continued, "May God give you strength to keep it."

Matt went to confession. He pledged not to drink for three months. He went to Mass and received communion for the first time in years. After three months—and then another six months—of not taking a drink, Matt made a lifelong pledge. It wasn't easy. He had no sponsors and no AA meetings for support. One day at church, he tried to walk forward to receive the Eucharist, but he couldn't move. "It's no use," a voice in his head told him. "You'll never stop drinking." Matt went to another church, and another, but the voice continued. Exhausted, Matt finally fell to his knees on the steps of a Dublin cathedral. He prayed aloud, "Jesus mercy, Mary help, Jesus mercy, Mary help."

Self-control: We can't do it alone

The voices disappeared, and Matt remained sober for the rest of his life. But temptations never left Matt. Soul-crushing poverty was still widespread in Dublin, and pubs on every street corner beckoned. In fact, most people received their pay inside those pubs!

Matt found strength in daily Mass. He read the Bible and the writings of Augustine and Francis de Sales. He repaid his drinking debts down to the last schilling. His natural generosity found its way back, and he shared everything he had. At work, whenever he had spare time, he prayed.

It wasn't until after Matt's death that people learned that the shabbily dressed man who walked to daily Mass had an incredibly rich and powerful inner life. Pope Paul VI declared him Venerable Matt Talbot, which is a step on the road to his canonization.

When Matt's mom prayed for him that evening long ago, she had to know that it was only with God's help that Matt could hold on. Superhuman strength was needed, and Matt got it—in the form of self-control that only comes from the Holy Spirit. His mom's prayer was answered.

Something to think about

Can you think of something that keeps you from living the full and happy life God intends for you? Maybe it's too much of something, like video gaming or tech devices or shopping. Maybe it's not enough of something, like prayer or getting to Mass or even a good night's sleep. Write down that thing here. Visualize the happy life you would lead if you could eliminate it (if it's bad) or get more of it (if it's good). Write down three ways you might change your behavior this week to get there.

_____

_____

_____

_____

Prayer

O God, the road ahead is long, and I can't see what's ahead.
Walk with me today. Show me what is good for me and what isn't.
And when I am too weak to resist temptation on my own, please carry
me in your arms. I know that with you I will get where I need to go.

19 Pedro Calungsod
THE ALMOST UNKNOWN MARTYR

Do you ever wonder about the millions of people in heaven who have never been officially declared saints? They could be your own ancestors, family, or friends. Maybe someone who once stood next to you in church or who drove past you in the car last week is now part of the communion of saints in heaven. Countless people have led lives of quiet faith or died martyr's deaths, yet we know little about them. They're probably fine with that. After all, they're enjoying the beatific vision. Those are the words we use to describe what can't be imagined—the unfathomable joy of the saints in the presence of the all-loving God.

Pedro Calungsod was one of those unknowns—until an old manuscript was unearthed that shed light on his short life. We know very little about Pedro, but a picture has gradually emerged of a teenager living in the Philippines in the seventeenth century. He joined a Jesuit missionary, Fr. Diego Luis de San Vitores, and became a catechist, preaching and teaching in what's now Guam. There, a rumor spread that they'd been poisoning people with baptismal water. (It didn't help when seriously ill people who were baptized actually died—from their illnesses.)

One day Fr. Diego and Pedro were on their way to baptize the newborn baby of an island leader, who barred their way. Fr. Diego tried to calm the leader down but it was no use. The leader was beside himself with anger. He wanted a confrontation with these missionaries on the spot, but he didn't have enough men to help. So he ran off searching for reinforcements. You can picture Fr. Diego and Pedro seeing the opening, looking at each other and maybe shrugging as they went on ahead. Fr. Diego baptized the baby girl, to the joy of her mom, who was a Christian. But when the chief returned and found a happy baptism celebration, he was not pleased.

He hurled spears at Pedro, who was fast and able to dodge them. In fact, Pedro had been an expert fighter who could have downed the chief in a second, but he was unarmed. One of the spears finally caught Pedro in the chest, and he went down. Fr. Diego quickly gave his young friend absolution and a final blessing before he too was killed with a spear.

After Pedro's death, the canonization process began, but the teenage catechist's cause became forgotten in the midst of political turmoil. It wasn't until 1981 that documents about Pedro were rediscovered. More than 300 years after his death, Pedro Calungsod was declared a saint by virtue of his martyrdom.

Purity of heart: A single-minded devotion to God

At Pedro's canonization, Pope St. John Paul II said that the teenager declared himself unwaveringly for Christ. That's what it means to have the Holy Spirit's chastity, or purity.

Sure, there's a sexual component, but that's only part of it. Chastity and purity are about something much bigger. People with pure hearts have no room inside for immorality, dishonor, or corruption. Like Pedro, they are single-minded in their love of God.

Something to think about
Jesus said, "Blessed are the pure of heart, for they will see God" (Matthew 5:8). Pedro Calungsod used his time to be a catechist. How do you spend your extra time? Is there something you might do during your free time to serve God better? Think about this and write your thoughts here.

_____

_____

_____

_____

Prayer
Jesus, I know that following you can be demanding.
Help me clear my head and heart of whatever is unworthy
of you. Give me the purity of heart that only comes from you.

20 You
YES, REALLY!

Surprise! The twentieth saint is...you! No, I'm not kidding.
In the Apostles' Creed, we say these words:

> *I believe in the Holy Spirit, the holy*
> *catholic Church, the communion of saints,*
> *the forgiveness of sins, the resurrection of*
> *the body, and the life everlasting.*

That communion of saints is the whole church, all the people—living and dead—who make up Christ's body. So as a baptized member of the church, you are, in a very real sense, a saint. But unlike the saints in this book, your story isn't finished. You have work ahead. So, here's your job. Start writing your own saint story on these pages. Write about something you've done that you think made God happy. (It's not bragging, really.) Write about something you did that maybe didn't make God happy, and what you will do to fix the situation. And think about your life ahead. The brilliant and the not-so-brilliant. The happy times and the sad times. Think about how you might use God's gifts, so that someday you can join the saints who say, "Honor, power, and might be to our God forever and ever" (Revelation 7:12). Amen! Alleluia!

Something to think about

Who do you know personally who is a model of the gifts and virtues of the Holy Spirit? Maybe it's a family member, a friend, coach, or teacher. Write about them here.

_____

_____

_____

_____

Prayer

Write your own prayer here. (Remember to praise and thank God for his great gifts to you.)

_____

_____

_____

_____

_____

_____

_____